Leader Lifestylez Vol. 2
Empower, Enable, and Enhance Leaders to Grow

L. Wayne Smalls

Copyright © 2018 L. Wayne Smalls

All rights reserved.

ISBN-10: 1978379935
ISBN-13: 978-1978379930

THANK YOU

I give thanks to God for giving me the inspiration to share my experiences with others in an effort to help them grow and become better people, as well as leaders. I dedicate this project to all of my family and friends who constantly support me and believe in my vision.

I would like to give a shout out to my team at L. Wayne Smalls & Associates, LLC who work tirelessly to help make the dream work. They understand the value of teamwork and that none of us can accomplish anything great all alone.

I would like to thank every mentor whose influence has helped me to become the man I am today. I've taken lessons and guidance from each one of them at different stages in my life that have helped propel me into becoming a lifelong learner of leadership.

CONTENTS

	Preface	Pg #3
1	**Empower**	Pg #6
	Explore Your Leadership Qualities	Pg #9
	Develop Your Communication Skills	Pg #13
	Leading Others by Example	Pg #17
	Empower Others to Be Good Team Players	Pg #23
2	**Enable**	Pg #29
	Increase Greatness. Help Your Followers Grow	Pg #35
3	**Enhance**	Pg #45
4	**Conclusion**	Pg #58
	About the Author	Pg #64

Preface

This is an attempt to describe the mindset behind the reinvented leadership as it was at the beginning of the 21st century, a mindset you could call conscious leadership. The mindset is the "tapestry on our walls," and hence provides the framing for our presence. This mindset is the omnipresent set of thoughts, paradigms, and philosophical approaches that we, the conscious leaders, base every action on. The mindset is nothing without actions. The actions are nothing without the mindset.

In this sense, leadership is a complex and multi-dimensional thing, covering philosophy, approach, daily governance, and interpersonal activities. Going forward the term leadership will cover all of this. Also, leadership is highly contextual, and will at times require a translation to the specific organization, leader, employees, type and scale of resources, skills, and competencies. You need to perform that translation to fit your needs as you read this. Hence, the mindset contains an infinite set of contextual mindsets, but with the same bearing points. Leadership is hard work. Leadership is demanding and takes time and slows you down until you've gotten the hang of it.

This book will discuss the responsibility of leaders to develop the people that follow them. Leaders must empower, enable, and enhance their followers to grow. Before this can happen, leaders must understand that their own growth process is what will control the level at which they can assist everyone around them to grow as well.

Empower

People who are talented are usually easy to recognize. Curiosity, intelligence, and determination tend to be noticeable in a crowd of ordinary people. In what ways do you nurture great potential when you discover it? After identifying specific talents in others, it can be simple to understand how to develop them based on their talents, as well as empower them as leaders. Unfortunately, many good potential leaders are overlooked by leadership because of their inability to quickly identify special talents. This can cause the potential leaders to get lost in the crowd, thereby slowing down their growth process and hindering the positive influence they could potentially have on others.

Leadership incorporates a variety of skills and qualities. A great leader can manage people and tasks, communicate effectively, and care for a positive team environment. Strive to build your leadership qualities. A good place to start is by evaluating your strengths and weaknesses. This will give you an idea of some of the things you do well. You can continue to do those things. You will gain an understanding of those things that may be weaknesses for you. You can create a plan to improve those things. Then, you can always work on setting a very good example to other people. Leadership can be a struggle to cultivate, as there are key qualities that are a little harder to nurture.

However, if you're inclined to face the task, and implement the guidelines that are listed in the pages that follow, you'll be on the right track to becoming the leader everyone will look up to.

Explore Your Leadership Qualities

Determine what kind of leader you really are. If you truly aspire to improve your leadership skills, it is very important that you honestly explore your strengths and weaknesses. As already mentioned, getting this done will allow you to pinpoint the areas you need to develop and make you more conscious of the way you act and behave. Start off by asking yourself, "what kind of leader am I? You must conduct self-assessments on a routine basis if you want to get an accurate account of where you are as a leader. These types of assessments are not to be taken lightly. You must really put the effort in and be honest with yourself. If used properly, they can be very useful to your growth and development. There are many assessment tools to choose from. The point is to pick any one that will give you the feedback you need.

Think of how other people might see you as a leader. Once you have determined what type of leader you are, it will be useful to find out how other people see you as a leader. You can seek input from your friends at school or college, or colleagues at work, accountability partners or mentors.

Explore your leadership qualities. After asking yourself the primary questions regarding the way you lead and how others see you, you can try to explore your leadership qualities in a more specific way. You can then choose which aspects you want to work on. Ask yourself the following questions and try to answer them as fairly as you can:

- Do I help other people perform at their best and achieve their fullest potential?

- Do I take responsibility?

- Can I communicate with others effectively?

- Am I an effective problem solver?

Recognize areas to develop. The above listed questions will assist you in highlighting which of the leadership qualities you are proficient in, and which of the qualities you need to build up. Making use of your answers to the questions, split your leadership qualities into three parts. First, take note of those qualities you think you are very effective at. Second, single out which areas require some improvement. Third, identify which areas are real weaknesses for you and require substantial attention.

Develop Your Communication Skills

Allow effective dialogue. Communication is perhaps one of the most significant leadership qualities, and one that runs within all the other vital qualities. One of the secrets to effective communication is allowing for positive and sometimes negative discussion on specific issues. There are various styles of leadership, but a leader who constantly shuts down debates and represses dialogue is not likely to maintain the support of other people for too long.

- Ask and encourage open questions, instead of constrictive questions.

- Draw attention to areas of agreement first and take care of the disagreements after that.

- Resist the urge to dominate every conversation! Instead, try to create an open environment where people are free to say what's on their mind without being intimidated.

Develop positive body language. Positive body language can assist you in coming across as positive, open, and supportive. It can also assist you in making a clear impression whenever you are speaking as well as improve the power and efficiency of your words. One rule of thumb is to develop body language that matches whatever message you are trying to communicate. Don't, for instance, ask somebody to get something done while you keep looking down at the floor. Rather, look the person in the eye while being open and pleasant.

To develop positive and favorable body language while talking, strive to maintain eye contact, stand straight, and try to relax your face. Your body language can be perceived as the way you are feeling, so attempt to display body language that replicates the qualities and class of a confident, positive leader.

Be an effective listener. To be an excellent communicator, you must be a great listener. If you try to listen to someone, she or he will notice that and come to think of you as someone they can talk to. This is a critical leadership quality to cultivate in your leadership style. Remember that your body language is vital, even when you are in listening mode. To be an effective listener:

- Refrain from judging.

- Give your undivided attention to whoever is talking to you.

- Attempt to understand others, before trying to make others understand you.

- Don't interrupt without a very good reason.

Leading Others by Example

Use creativity. One feature of good leadership is the ability to think quickly and move to action to provide sound solutions to problems. If you realize something needs to be done and you are certain that you understand the best way to get it done, make use of your creativity. A great leader is ready to take the initiative in all types of situations without being asked to do so. Making use of your creativity shows a positive, "can do" attitude. Be confident in your actions, always. Act progressively with self-assurance, and don't try to rush to a solution when the problem calls for further discussion. It takes a good leader to recognize when it is time to take action, or when a problem demands further research before it can be tackled.

Have a mentor. No matter the situation, it is always advantageous when you have someone to look up to who possesses superb, resilient leadership competencies. It makes life so much easier to see someone's works in action rather than living by words written on paper.

Rarely will someone ask to be your mentor – you will probably have to initiate that conversation unless it is a current friend or a relative. A mentor could possibly be anyone you respond. To have a good mentor-protege relationship, though, it helps if you can find someone who is in the same industry that you are in. Observe potential mentors who have related values, then have occasional meetings with them to determine who you have the best connection with and can learn the most from. Be ready to give details of what you wish to learn, why you respect their perspective, leadership ability, and what you can bring to the relationship.

When confronted with a difficult decision, imagine the way your mentor would deal with it. Consider what they've done to be successful in the past. Consider what your mentor has shared with you. This can help you select the right course of action when you find yourself facing difficult times.

Take responsibility. To establish yourself as a strong example of a leader, it is very important that you take full responsibility for your individual duties and priorities as well as that of your entire team, group, or organization. Having well-defined priorities and distinctly assigned roles will set the stage for people to recognize and own their responsibilities. Help your team members to accomplish their tasks and try to build a cooperative culture rather than a competitive culture and environment. Taking responsibility can also involve temporarily relieving an individual of responsibilities if they have proven that they are not yet ready to handle. They may require further training; therefore, it will be up to you to ensure they receive it.

Continue developing your skills. One way

to display good leadership skills is to always be prepared for new possibilities to acquire and develop your competencies. Showing a constant desire to develop yourself can inspire those around you. It shows your commitment to excellence and your unwillingness to settle for complacency.

Give a vision. A great leader is someone who can give a clear and concise vision for the short and longer term. The wisdom to see into the future, think strategically, and build priorities are all characteristics of strong and great leaders. To do this, you will have to broaden your scope of things so that you can see the bigger picture. Imagining the bigger picture can help you foresee problems before they ever happen. This method of thinking can also bring about innovation and fundamental changes that have long term values.

Empower Others to Be Good Team Players

Inspire others. For great teamwork, you need motivated partners. One of the most effective ways for a leader to inspire colleagues is to pay full attention to them and make it clear that you are there to offer support and assist them when necessary. Try to have people concentrate on goals that have the highest priority, providing a clear way forward. You shouldn't be the very last person to learn if someone is struggling or is dealing with something that could prevent them from accomplishing their goals. Commit yourself to being involved enough to recognize problems and sort them out before they become bigger problems. This might involve adjusting your team or the distribution of work within the team. For instance, if a member of the team is losing interest because they may not feel challenged enough, think of different ways you can get them engaged and excited about being a contributing team member. You could give details of how this work, though it may be a bit boring, is crucial to the whole project.

Show resolve in all your decisions. When you take on the responsibility of leadership, you are expected to be comfortable making tough decisions and then sticking to those decisions. You can't be terrified to be decisive and make hard calls when situations call for it.

Praise good work. A crucial part of inspiring other people is praising good work. Look for chances to compliment people for a job well done and show them that you appreciate all they are doing. Taking a keen interest in your colleagues' work is a crucial attribute of a good leader who can inspire a team. Always be on the watch for career development prospects. A positive working culture where people's productivity is valued and appreciated will bring about an even more inspired group.

Work as a team rather than as competitors. If you are aiming to be a great leader, you may unintentionally create a competitive environment between other people or even your coworkers. You must try to avoid this as much as possible. It may be better to focus on building a more cooperative work environment, which often leads to more valuable and dependable working relationships. Any controversy that comes up in a competitive culture can cost precious time and resources to sort out. You are better off building common goals that you can accomplish collectively. Building a cooperative environment will strengthen relationships and help individuals to steer clear of working in a vacuum.

Be approachable and welcoming. If you are a leader leading a team on a project, it is very important that you are accessible to them. Bear in mind that a great leader is someone who not only gets the task done, but is also involved with assisting colleagues with their development and helping them reach their fullest potential. Make yourself available to mentoring younger people and be sure to create time for one-to-one training when necessary.

Be Passionate. Would you look to someone for support and leadership if they did not really care about you or your dreams? Obviously not! Great leaders are not just absorbed with getting group members to complete specific tasks in the workplace; they also have an honest desire to see their people be successful in all areas.

You can build this leadership quality by coming up with different ways to demonstrate your zeal for others. Let people see that you are concerned about their progress. When one person communicates something with the rest of the group members, be sure to express how much you value their input.

Who says leadership is a one-way relationship? It certainly is not. As you work towards developing these leadership traits, remember to look to each one of your followers for feedback. Take note of the things that have been effective in the past and constantly be on the lookout for new methods to inspire every group member.

Enable

Leaders have the honor and the responsibility to add value to their teams and organizations. The size of the organization is irrelevant—a leader is there to "raise the tide so all boats float higher". When that happens, employees are challenged, they feel valued, and are more productive, more innovative and more likely to help the company achieve great success. Leaders who add real value to their organizations incorporate the following beliefs and behaviors into their daily routine:

1. Be a real leader. Sounds simple, but if it was so simple, the world, every country, every state and city would be a much better place. When faced with complexity and chaos, we have a tendency to revert back to our comfort zones. In other words, we may spend more time working in the functional areas that we are most familiar with. It makes us feel productive, but it doesn't move the organization forward. As a leader, if you are not focusing on the future of the company, where it is going, and how it is going to get there, who is?

2. Employ the right people for the right jobs. The companies we admire, the ones that do well in bad times and good, hire the right people. Brett Blair, owner of Sanford Rose Associates in Michigan, will confirm that finding the right candidate is too important to take lightly. It starts with very clear requirements and a strong emphasis on matching values to the company culture. How do you know if you have the right people? Many companies like Zappos and Southwest Airlines have unique hiring processes that support their cultural norms. Zappos tries to hire the best, trains them for two weeks and then offers them $2,000 to leave! They want commitment. Many successful companies will tell you that prior industry experience is not only less important than skills and style, but in some cases (like a bank that is trying to be less "banky"), a hindrance.

3. Positive attitude. How do leaders expect their associates to come to work every day and be productive if they don't know if they will have a job tomorrow? A leader not only has to have a "great day" every day while at work, but they also offer hope. Rick Frost, CEO of LP Construction says, "giving employees hope means that they can focus on their work, not worry about their immediate future." Most companies that come out of recessions successfully do not have a major layoff or repeated ones, but focus on productivity improvements that drop margin to the bottom line and leave employees knowing where they stand.

4. Be transparent. A leader needs to lead with consistency. How they make decisions, the values they cherish, the expectations they hold have to be made known to employees if they are expected to excel.

5. Develop people. As Joe Scarlett, founder of the Scarlett Leadership Institute says, the sure fire way to success is having great talent around you. As a leader, your job is to let them shine. Many successful leaders make a point of hiring people smarter than they are with a different perspective that challenges them, and all agree they don't want "yes men" on staff. By developing people in your organization to this level of greatness, the organization becomes great. This is one of the key principles in Jim Collins' book, *Good to Great*. It is about getting the "right seats on the bus."

6. Have a vision. A leader's job is to lead. Thus, there must be a place in mind that you are journeying to. Be sure that your vision is shared, clear, and memorable. Repeat it often and reward those who are moving the company in that direction, and as a team, you will get there faster than you may think.

If leaders is spending their time on these pursuits, the employees win and, of course, so does the company. Any organization is as strong as its weakest link—as a leader, if you strengthen the links, you strengthen the company. Stay focused on these important tasks. As a leader it is your responsibility. If you do, you will add significant value to your team members and your organization and you will be viewed as an outstanding leader.

Increase Greatness. Help Your Followers Grow

Any leader who values improvements and progress would understand the great advantage involved with working with a team that tends to grow as fast as the speed of light. Growth and learning new things are elements that attracts an individual to become a great leader, and a good leader to become an iconic one. For one to be known as a successful leader, others must have grown through him or her. Jack Welch says, "Before you are a leader, success is all about growing yourself. When you become a leader, success is all about growing others."

But the ultimate question is: How do you as a leader help your followers grow? Just like many other intellectual questions, it doesn't have a definite answer. But these next few concepts will shed light on ways it can be achieved.

1. Lead by Example. This must be the first. A leader who strives to see improvements in his staff wouldn't just sit in his office, barking out orders and punishments. A good leader would be one whose actions would force everyone to do that which is right to enhance personal growth and development. If you want your team to exude excellence, then you must first exude excellence yourself. That behavior you expect from your team should be the one you demonstrate.

2. Support New Ideas. How do you expect your followers to avoid being stagnant if you push their innovations and ideas off the table? People tend to lose motivation if their ideas are constantly shut down. The more you shut down suggestions and improvements from your team, the harder it becomes for them to come up with better ones. Great leaders know the importance of involving the team, and making good use of their ideas, giving them credit if they work out well and continuing to encourage them when they don't go so well. This way, followers gain confidence in their abilities and they can elevate to take on more responsibilities.

3. Utilize the Power of Words. Eugene Peterson

translates a passage from the Bible in James chapter 3 in this way, "A word out of your mouth may seem of no account, but it can accomplish nearly anything-- or destroy it!" These words capture the truth in twenty words, more accurately than ever. As a leader, your words should hold immense power. When you appreciate members of your team, they should understand that you absolutely mean it. Your words should build people up, not tear them apart. After a job well done, let them know you are proud of them and happy about the completed project. Most importantly, make them understand that they can even do better; that next time they'll do an even better job. Matt McWilliams identifies four magic leadership words: "I believe in you." These words have more effects on the human mind than many other words of encouragement.

4. Preach Hope, Not Fear. Dwight Eisenhower, the 34th President of the United States once said, "You don't lead by hitting people on the head-- that's assault, not leadership." When you use more of the stick rather than the carrot, people will do the 'least amount possible to avoid the whip.' When your team is unhappy and stressed out than focused and goal-driven, there isn't a single way you can enhance their growth, which inadvertently is going to affect you; the leader. When you use the carrot instead of the stick, people will step out of their comfort zone to make things happen. They will do things they may have thought impossible in past times. Breathe hope into the members of your team. This way, they will try to work to meet your positive expectations, making them improve themselves in the process.

5. Ask Questions. As a leader, the best way to get to the truth of any matter is to ask questions. An inquisitive leader keeps the members on their feet, knowing that questions could pop up any time as to the reasons for their actions. Also, it motivates the team in the sense that they believe their path has been well considered.

6. Encourage Personal Development. Most people will work better when they realize you, the leader, is more interested in matters other than your output. Great leaders take part in the personal battles of their members, offer valuable advice, and help them get to their victory. When you show genuine interest in their personal development, they will work harder and better all in a effort to satisfy you.

7. Set Realistic Goals. One of the letters in the SMART acronym is the "R" which stands for Realistic. A goal that isn't realistic is one that may never become fruitful because it is being done at the wrong time, with the wrong resources. Set achievable goals; one which people can make possible if they work hard enough. People cannot grow if you continue throwing them against the wall. At the end of the day, after the goal comes to fruition, let the man or woman of the moment celebrate the win.

8. Let There Be Discipline. If a certain member makes a mistake, or fails to deliver on an agreed deadline, it has the power to demotivate the rest of the team. There must be disciplinary actions for non-compliance to clearly defined rules. It should be fairly handled if a certain member breaks the rules. There should be consequences, as consequences are needed to make members work and act upright. Everyone in the team, group, or organization must be held accountable for their actions or inactions.

9. Feedback. How do you expect people to know if they are not performing to standard if you, the leader, fail to provide helpful feedback? Leaders should point out errors and suggest ways it can be rectified, and how to avoid them the next time. But most importantly, a leader should be specific. Being vague and ambiguous will only frustrate people and possibly cause them to lose faith in themselves and you as the leader. Feedback can also be positive. Giving positive feedback allows individuals to know what they are doing well. Naturally, actions that are positive should be repeated. Besides, who doesn't want to hear that they are doing a good job. It is motivation to keep going and possibly becoming even better.

10. Offer Challenges. People tend to be too comfortable or complacent making the chances for improvements a little tight. A good leader pushes his team members or followers out of their comfort zones. He nudges them to push their limits, to expand their potential. When they are successful, as a leader, you should celebrate their breakthrough. Also, when they fail, encourage them to try again, this time with renewed energy.

Enhance

Ten steps to enhancing your leadership skills

"The miracle power that elevates the few is to be found in their industry, application, and perseverance, under the promptings of a brave determined spirit." **— Mark Twain**

Many motivational experts like to say that leaders are made, not born. It can be argued either way. I believe we are all born with some natural leadership abilities. Some people nurture those abilities. Some people are deprogrammed along the way. As children, we were natural leaders - curious and humble, always hungry and thirsty for knowledge, with an incredibly vivid imagination. We knew exactly what we wanted. We were persistent and determined in getting what we wanted, and had the ability to motivate, inspire, and influence everyone around us to help us in accomplishing our mission. So why is this so difficult to do as adults? What happened? As children, over time, we got used to hearing, "No," "Don't," and "Can't." "No!" Don't do this! Don't do that! You can't do this. You can't do that. "No!" Many of our parents told us to keep quiet and not disturb the adults by asking silly questions. This pattern continued into high school with our teachers telling us what we could do and couldn't do and what was possible. Many of us got hit with the big one – institutionalized formal education known as college. Unfortunately, the traditional educational system doesn't teach students how to become leaders; it teaches students how to become polite order takers for the corporate world. Instead of learning to become creative, independent, self-reliant, and think for themselves, most people learn how to obey and intelligently follow rules to keep the corporate machine humming. Developing the leader in you to live your highest life, requires a process of 'unlearning' by self-remembering and self-honoring. Being an effective leader again will require you to be brave and unlock the door to your inner attic, where your childhood dreams lie, going inside to the heart.

Based on my several years of experience in the area of leadership, here are ten easy steps you can take to awaken the leader in you and rekindle your passion for greatness:

1. Humility. Leadership starts with humility. To be a highly successful leader, you must first humble yourself like a child and be willing to serve others. Nobody wants to follow someone who is arrogant. Be humble – always curious, always hungry and thirsty for knowledge. What is excellence but knowledge plus knowledge plus knowledge - always wanting to better yourself, always improving, always growing. When you are humble, you become genuinely interested in people because you want to learn from them. When you want to learn and grow, you will be a far more effective listener, which is the #1 leadership communication tool. When people sense you are genuinely interested in them, and listening to them, they will naturally be interested in you and listen to what you have to say as well.

2. SWOT Yourself. SWOT is an acronym for Strengths, Weaknesses, Opportunities, and Threats. Although it's a strategic management tool taught at Stanford and Harvard Business Schools and used by large multi-nationals, it can just as effectively be used in your own professional development as a leader. This is a useful key to gain access to self-knowledge, self-remembering, and self-honoring. Start by listing your strengths including your accomplishments. Then write down all your Weaknesses and what needs to be improved. Make sure to include any doubts, anxieties, fears, and worries that you may have. These are the demons and dragons guarding the door to your inner attic. By bringing them to conscious awareness, you can begin to slay them. Then proceed on to list all the Opportunities you see available to you for using your strengths. Finally, write down all the Threats or obstacles that are currently blocking you or that you think you will encounter along the way to achieving your dreams.

3. Follow Your Passion. Regardless of how busy you are, always take time to do what you love doing. Being a lively and positive person vitalizes others. When you are pursuing your passions, people around you cannot help but feel impassioned by your presence. This will make you a magnetic leader. Whatever it is that you enjoy doing, be it writing, acting, painting, drawing, photography, sports, reading, dancing, networking, or working on entrepreneurial ventures, set aside time every week, to pursue these activities. Believe me, you'll find the time. If you were to video tape yourself for a day, you would be shocked to see how much time goes to waste!

4. Dream Big. If you want to be larger than life, you need a dream that's larger than life. Small dreams won't serve you or anyone else. It takes the same amount of time to dream small than it does to dream big. So be big and be bold! Write down your one biggest dream - the one that excites you the most. Remember, don't be small and realistic in this drill! Be bold and unrealistic! Go for the gold, the Pulitzer, the Nobel, the Oscar, the highest you can possibly achieve in your field. After you've written down your dream, list every single reason why you CAN achieve your dream instead of worrying about why you can't.

5. Intuition. Without intuition, we can perish. If you can't see yourself winning that award and feel the tears of triumph streaming down your face, it's unlikely you will be able to lead yourself or others to victory. You must be able to visualize what it would be like accomplishing your dream. See it, smell it, taste it, hear it, feel it in your gut.

6. Perseverance. Victory belongs to those who want it the most and stay in it the longest. Now that you have a dream, make sure you take consistent action every day. I recommend doing at least 5 things every day that will move you closer to your dream. Commit to it and never quit.

7. Honor Your Word. Every time you break your word, you lose power and trust. Successful leaders keep their word and their promises. You can accumulate all the toys and riches in the world, but you only have one reputation in life. Your word is gold. Honor it!

8. Be a Mentor. As a leader, you should be a mentor to those who follow you. As someone who has already achieved a high degree of success in your field, you should make a well-qualified mentor for a few people. There are excellent mentoring websites and great resources for finding local mentoring programs. They even have free personal profiles that you can fill out in order to potentially find suitable proteges to guide. Remember, there will be people who are in search of a good mentor, so remember to make yourself available. Be willing to share books of great leaders that you admire. Your proteges will appreciate you for that.

9. Be Yourself. Use your relationships with mentors and your research on great leaders as models or reference points to work from, but never copy or imitate them. Everyone has vastly different leadership styles. History books are filled with leaders who are soft-spoken, introverted, and quiet, all the way to the other extreme of being outspoken, extroverted, and loud, and everything in between. A quiet and simple Gandhi or a soft-spoken peanut farmer named Jimmy Carter, who became president of the United States and won a Nobel Peace Prize, have been just as effective world leaders as a loud and flamboyant Churchill, or the tough leadership style employed by 'The Iron Lady,' Margaret Thatcher. I admire Ernest Hemingway as a writer. However, if I copy Hemingway, I'd be a second or third rate Hemingway, at best, but in doing that, I would not be a first rate Wayne. Be yourself, your best self, always competing against yourself and bettering yourself, and you will become a first rate YOU instead of a second rate somebody else.

10. Give. Finally, be a giver. Leaders are givers. By giving, you activate a universal law as sound as gravity: 'life gives to the giver, and takes from the taker.' The more you give, the more you get. If you want more love, respect, support, and compassion, give love, give respect, give support, and give compassion. Be a mentor to others. Give back to your community. As a leader, the only way to get what you want, is by helping enough people get what they want first. As Sir Winston Churchill once said, "We make a living by what we get, we make a life by what we give."

The core principles of leadership for everyone include articulating a vision, think and act strategically, act decisively, communicate persuasively, motivate the troops, build relationships, and building leadership in others. Of course, these need to be customized for every culture and every business environment and organization. In every environment, there is a final and most vital leadership principle – common purpose comes first and personal self-interest comes last.

Leadership has its greatest impact in times of uncertainty and change, like the present. How wide is your knowing-doing gap, and how actively are you working to activate it?

Conclusion

Leadership is hard work.

Leadership is demanding and takes time and slows you down until you have get the hang of it. Leadership is also rewarding, immensely giving, and attractive, and once you have "tasted the kool-aid," you just want more.

Leadership may not be for everyone.

I have met people that never could work this way, because they chose not to. They don't want to put the time and effort into doing this. That is what makes someone say, "I'm not a leader." The successful leaders I have met are hard working, people-oriented, result-oriented, gentle, engaging, empathetic leaders, who you would dedicate enormous amounts of time too. I hope you'll be inspired because going to work should be nice, great, and awesome. However, leadership is not only for your 9-5 job; it is a lifestyle. Leadership is a part of your approach to everyone; your family, your parents, your children, your spouse, in traffic, in sports, in politics, in the grocery store, when making music, online and offline.

Leadership is a choice

Engaging in true leadership is an active, deliberate, conscious choice. People may be born with natural ability, but they still must make a choice whether they will put in the work required to be great leaders who can influence others to be great as well.

Leadership is about people

Leadership is about trust, respect, safety, and well-being, and it will make people thrive. Leadership is about releasing the power to yourself, the individual, and the team by acknowledging each other's existence, approach, and opinion. Leadership is about believing in others and seeing the value in them. I can only be my best when you are at your best. We strive to make each other exceed our dreams.

Leadership is about authenticity

Be yourself at all times. Be human. Don't leave your identity at the doorstep when you go to work. Strive to be the same in all situations at home, at work, and everywhere else. If you change your leadership style from situation to situation, you will lose people' s trust in you.

Leadership is about emotions

A leadership culture embraces emotions, beliefs, and opinions. A leader should be empathetic and have sympathy, and must strive to understand strengths and flaws, both in ourselves and our colleagues.

Leadership is visionary and ambitious

A leader creates visions and dreams and engages both himself/herself and the organization in them. A leader is ambitious, both personally and on behalf of others.

Leadership is about purpose

Rallying for a cause with great energy and determination is a fundamental part of leadership. Engaging people with and for a purpose and vision is the strongest catalyst for commitment, great results, and productivity, while still nurturing overall well-being. It is about ensuring that every action in the team supports the purpose and is meaningful. You need to know why you go to work. It has to make sense to you, your team, for your product, for the organization, and for the customers. If it doesn't make sense, then stop! A leader sets the direction and explains the purpose (WHY). A leader provides tools (HOW).

A leader provides clear demands, requirements, expectations, directions, and framing (WHAT and WHEN and WHO).

ABOUT THE AUTHOR

Independent certified speaker, Amazon Best Selling author, L Wayne Smalls became a resident of Fayetteville, NC. after serving over 25 years of total service in the United States Army; he retired at the rank of Major. Some of Wayne's military awards include a Bronze Star Medal for combat in Afghanistan, the Army Commendation Medal, the Joint Service Achievement Medal and many others. He also has an extensive professional educational background in business administration and leadership development.

Wayne is the president and founder of L. Wayne Smalls & Associates LLC., a leadership training and consulting company that assists individuals and organizations in empowering, enabling and enhancing leaders to grow. The goal of the company is to provide high quality professional training that can improve the overall effectiveness of any organization. Some of the services that are provided are keynotes, motivational speeches leadership coaching and training, team building workshops, seminars and mastermind groups.

With a climbing number of progressive books and publications, Wayne is noted for the Amazon #1 Best Seller, "Called to Be a Soldier". Not only is Wayne an author; but he is certified and mentored by John C. Maxwell, the number one leadership guru in the world. As a steward of leadership and inspiration, Wayne believes that everyone can reach their fullest potential with the proper guidance, motivation and inspiration.

Wayne is the host of his own leadership talk radio show, Leader Lifestylez, which airs on WIDU 1600 AM every Monday at 9:00am. Wayne is a part of several mentoring groups in the community and has a strong passion for helping others to achieve their dreams.